Love for Her Sistas
Poems to Uplift, Empower & Inspire Women

Valencia Clay

Love for Her Sistas

Poems to Uplift, Empower & Inspire Women

Valencia Clay

Love for Her Sistas
Poems to Uplift, Empower & Inspire Women

ISBN: 9780692943205
Copyright © 2016 by Valencia Clay
Published by: V.L.C. House of Self-Help Publishing

Printed in the United States of America

Love for Her Sistas

Poems to Empower, Uplift & Inspire Women

V.L.C. House of Self-Help Publishing

Dedication

Thank you God for blessing me with the words of wisdom to connect and share with our most precious Sistas! You have always been there for me through the good and bad times. Thank you for giving me a purpose in life. Thank you for never leaving my side when I felt alone and lost. Thank you Father God for showering me with unconditional love. Most importantly, thank you for being the best support system ever. You continue to open doors and I am forever grateful.

Love you always!!!

Table of Contents

Introduction

I wrote this collection of poems to inspire our Sistas in the world. No matter what you're going through and no matter what your circumstances are, you must never ever give up. Certainly, you will face obstacles, challenges and adversities, not to break you down but to build you up and make you stronger. Sista, you are a Woman of God with powers beyond measure. When life throws you a curveball, tap into your Divine Powers and hit a homerun. Within you are Divine Powers of infinite possibilities, love, courage, compassion, kindness, peace, harmony and prosperity. Your mind is a powerful tool that can create and manifest. You can create greatness if you believe in the power to be great. Take your powers back and claim what belongs to you. I hope this book of poems inspires you to move forward regardless of your circumstances.

Be Strong and Keep the faith! Love and Light!

God Bless!

SHE'S A WOMAN OF ACTION

SHE'S A WOMAN OF ACTION

She's a woman with choices, it gives her great satisfaction,

In her faith she rejoices, she's a woman of action.

Her focus is steady, left out are distractions,

She's willing and ready, she's a woman of action.

She walks with a purpose that fuels her inner passions,

Community is her service, she's a woman of action.

Compassion and love is her secret attraction,

Love is what she dreams of, she's a woman of action.

She walks with such a grace, stylish and fashion,

And moves at her own pace, she's a woman of action.

Negativity passed down like it's a chain reaction,

She still wears her Crown because she's a woman of action.

What spurs you into a Women of Action?

_____

_____

_____

_____

_____

_____

_____

_____

_____

_____

_____

_____

Now ACTIVATE and go after your Passions!

LIVING HER DREAMS

LIVING HER DREAMS

She wakes up every morning, pours her coffee and cream,

Then she leaps into action towards living her dreams.

Her focus is sharp, sharper than a laser beam,

She will do what it takes to start living her dreams.

It flows through her body, like it's in her bloodstream,

She loves to live life, life is about living her dreams.

Purpose gives her hope and it boosts her self-esteem,

She knows how to cope before giving up on her dreams.

Patiently she waits, no matter how long it may seem,

Nothing could go wrong when it comes to living her dreams.

Challenges she's faced but keeps swimming upstream,

Her dreams she loves to chase until she's living her dreams.

Confident in every way, to have God on her team,

That someday, just one day she will go on living her dreams.

Lists some of the dreams that you want to achieve!

_____

_____

_____

_____

_____

_____

_____

_____

_____

_____

_____

_____

_____

_____

One step at a time, get out there and achieve them!

HER HEAD UP HELD HIGH

HER HEAD UP HELD HIGH

She's faced many obstacles as time passes by,

But she always walks with her head up held high.

Many times she's fallen down, in her troubles she cry,

And still gets back up with her head up held high.

If she fails at something, she continues to try,

And she keeps on walking with her head up held high.

She knows it takes courage to spread her wings and fly,

Never is she discouraged but keeps her head up held high.

She rejoices in God, lifting her hands up to the sky,

And it's her job to keep her head up held high.

She goes through her struggles and refuses to ask why,

No matter the troubles, she chooses to walk with her head up held high.

How do you feel when you walk with your head held high?

_____

_____

_____

_____

_____

_____

_____

_____

_____

_____

_____

*Regardless of Your Circumstances,
always walk with your head held high!*

A CONFIDENT WOMAN

A CONFIDENT WOMAN

A confident woman is determined to win,

She has a beauty that shines within her own skin.

She knows what she wants and goes after her dreams,

She's a confident woman with high self-esteem.

A confident woman lives with faith in her heart,

She's confident to step up and do her own part.

A confident woman doesn't have to shout loud,

She exudes enough confidence to stand out in the crowd.

Times she will rise and times she might fall,

A confident woman gets back up and stand tall.

A confident woman makes her own power moves,

She does what it takes for her life to improve.

A confident woman keeps her head to the skies,

A confident woman is always on the RISE!

Lists what makes you a Confident Woman!

_____

_____

_____

_____

_____

_____

_____

_____

_____

_____

_____

_____

_____

Now be confident in the woman you are!

A SISTA ALWAYS HAS A PLAN

A SISTA ALWAYS HAS A PLAN

A Sista who believes, believes that she can,

She's wants to achieve and she always has a plan.

She faces her fears with integrity she stands,

Her fears disappear and sets in motion her plan.

She doesn't seek approvals but admired are her fans,

She's her own individual and she always has a plan.

She enjoys helping others and lends a helping hand,

For the love of her Sistas, she always has a plan.

She leaps with great faith and on her feet she lands,

That's the kind of Sista, who always has a plan.

Her visions in life, are larger than grand,

Decisions, decisions, this Sista always has a plan.

To trust in her God and do as He commands,

Even against the odds, she's a Sista with a plan.

Lists your goals that you want to accomplish!

_____

_____

_____

_____

_____

_____

_____

_____

_____

_____

_____

*Create a plan, take it step by step
and make it happen!*

Woman of Courage

WOMAN OF COURAGE!

No matter how many strikes, no matter how many blows,

She's a woman of courage,

Courage is the only thing she knows.

Challenges may come, challenges may go,

She's a woman of courage,

Courage is the only thing she knows.

She reaps what she sows, she blossoms, she grows,

She's a woman of courage,

Courage is the only thing she knows.

She goes with the wind, as the wind blows, she flows,

She's a woman of courage,

Courage is the only thing she knows.

Her confidence glows, in a room it shows,

She's a woman of courage,

Courage is the only thing she knows.

What are some challenges faced and overcame!

_____

_____

_____

_____

_____

_____

_____

_____

_____

_____

_____

Now celebrate your victories!

Commitment to Self-Love

COMMITMENT TO SELF-LOVE

Love is who I am, Love is all I see,

I can be whatever it is that I want to be.

Self-Love grows within like a fruitful tree,

Isn't *Self-Love* beautiful, wouldn't you agree?

Everything about myself, I love it all completely,

I'm committed to *Self-Love* because *Self-Love* is my responsibility.

Freedom is *Self-Love* and *Self-Love* makes me free,

Self-Love makes me happy and my happiness is key.

I'm committed to *Self-Love* because I LOVE me some ME,

I love all of myself faithfully and unconditionally.

Self-Love I express with potential and capabilities,

I'm committed to *Self-Love* and *Self-Love* is all I see.

What does Self-Love mean you?

_____

_____

_____

_____

_____

_____

_____

_____

_____

_____

_____

_____

_____

_____

Use these statements as your daily affirmations

Her God Knows Best

HER GOD KNOWS BEST

She doesn't need to worry, she doesn't need to stress,

She puts her trust in God because Her God knows best.

She counts her blessings and worries are less,

No reason to doubt because Her God knows best.

She travels with passion on her mission and quest,

God moves her to action because Her God knows best.

She learns her lessons through mistakes and through tests,

She's destined for greatness because Her God knows best.

She settles for greater and will never settles for less,

She chooses sooner than later because Her God knows best.

Her mind is at peace, a peaceful mind she invests,

The negativity is released because Her God knows best.

She believes in her dreams and her dreams will manifest,

With God on team, she trusts in Him who knows best.

Lists what makes God great in your life!

_____

_____

_____

_____

_____

_____

_____

_____

_____

_____

_____

Always appreciate what God has done!

She Puts Her Ego Aside

SHE PUTS HER EGO ASIDE

Her true self she lives, it's not something she hides,

She's true to herself and she puts her Ego aside.

Love, compassion and kindness within her resides,

Has taught her how to put her Ego aside.

Getting in the way, will never be her pride,

She would rather pray to God and put her Ego aside.

The Ego only wrecks and it's not a joyful-ride,

She put her Ego in-check then puts her Ego aside.

The Ego separates and the Ego divides,

She does what it takes and put her Ego aside.

What grows is God's trust, in her faith she confides,

She knows that she must, put her Ego aside.

How can the Ego have a negative effect on your life?

_____

_____

_____

_____

_____

_____

_____

_____

_____

_____

Now try and keep your Ego in check!

She Will Never Ever Quit!

SHE WILL NEVER EVER QUIT

She does what it takes, to her goals she commits,

She will never give up and she will never ever quit.

The past she doesn't dwell but quickly gets over it,

Her story she tells, why she will never ever quit.

She counts her blessings, more than a just little bit

It teaches her lessons to never, ever quit.

To wants to be a winner, she has to admit,

Winners never give up and she will never ever quit.

When times get rough, she doesn't throw a fit,

She knows how to be tough and she will never ever quit.

She surrenders to God and to God she submits,

Because God is her defender, she will never ever quit.

What makes you a Winner and not a Quitter?

_____

_____

_____

_____

_____

_____

_____

_____

_____

_____

_____

Stay Winning and don't ever Quit!

Her Twin Soul

HER TWIN SOUL

The first day they met, things spun out of control,

She will never forget the day she met her Twin Soul.

He captured her heart and his heart she stole,

She will never forget the day she met her Twin Soul.

She found a great treasure as if she's struck gold,

She will never forget the day she met her Twin Soul.

Her thoughts every night in her mind she would hold,

Him holding her tight, in love mind, body and soul.

So brave, so bold, as one, separate but whole,

She will be never forget the day she met her Twin Soul.

A happy ending, no regrets, she's accomplished her goal,

She will never forget the day she met her Twin Soul.

Lists some great qualities of your Ideal Mate!

_____

_____

_____

_____

_____

_____

_____

_____

_____

_____

_____

Now see these qualities in yourself and you will attract what you see in yourself!

We All Make Mistakes

WE ALL MAKE MISTAKES

Bad choices we make, life isn't perfect or great,

But give yourself a break, we all make mistakes.

Love who you are, love others and not hate,

You've made it this far, we all make mistakes.

Just be a better you and it's never too late,

Whatever you go through, we all make mistakes.

No one is perfect, in our differences we relate,

Keep our judgments in-check, we all make mistakes.

Trials and errors we learn but not to seal our own fate,

Life has its twist and turns, we all make mistakes.

Look up to one another, encourage and motivate,

Because when it's all said and done, we all make mistakes.

What are some mistakes you've made in the past?

_____

_____

_____

_____

_____

_____

_____

_____

_____

_____

Learn from these mistake and try
Not to repeat them again!

She's Ready to Rise!

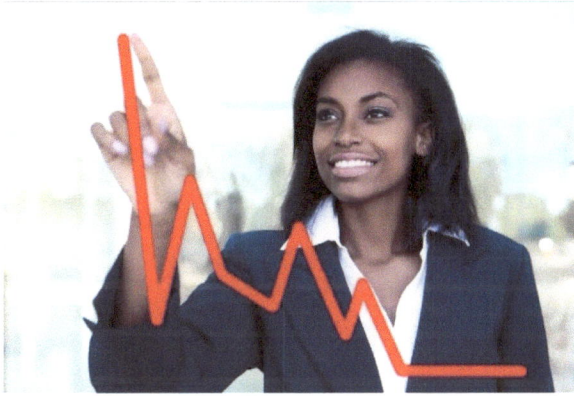

SHE'S READY TO RISE

She will never give up, no matter how many tries,

She's bold, she tough, she's ready to RISE.

She looks at her chances with a sparkle in her eyes,

Regardless of her circumstances, she stay ready to RISE.

Faithful to God is where her trust lies,

She wants to get the job done and she's ready to RISE.

She reaches for her goals, she keeps her head to the skies,

She knows God is in control, she's ready to RISE.

The challenges she's faced are like blessings in disguise,

Time she doesn't waste because she's ready to RISE.

What would you like to see Women Rise above?

_____

_____

_____

_____

_____

_____

_____

_____

_____

_____

_____

_____

Now, go out and set a positive example that you want to see in the world!

CALL HER THE QUEEN

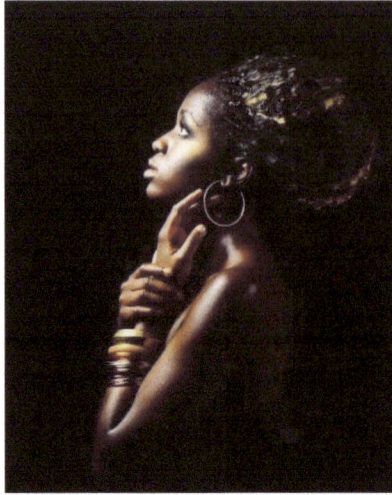

CALL HER THE QUEEN

She's focused on her goals just like a laser-beam,

Her goals become dreams, you can call her the Queen.

Hard works she puts in, while God works behind the scenes,

God's blessings He sends, you can call her the Queen.

Through the ups and downs, she dances in between,

She knows God is around, you can call her the Queen.

Supporters loves her passion, they become part of the team,

She's admired for her actions, you can call her the Queen.

She's made some wrong turns until God intervenes,

Her lessons are learned and you can call her the Queen.

What makes a Queen a Queen!

_____

_____

_____

_____

_____

_____

_____

_____

_____

_____

_____

Now Crown Yourself for Being a Queen!

Message to My Beautiful Sistas:

Blessings Sistas! I hope my collection of poems have inspired you today. I want you to remember how special and deserving you are. You deserve happiness, success, prosperity, love, peace, harmony, blessings, joy, abundance and greatness.

It's important to encourage and inspire all women because we are all ONE. It is important to build each other up with words to inspire. You never know what the next woman is going through. Words are powerful and they could hurt or heal. We should use our words to uplift and not tear one another down. We all face challenges in life and if we could be more understanding, accepting and tolerant of our differences, there would be less jealousy, envy, competition and comparison.

Let's be more compassionate and kind towards one another. Let's open our heart and spread the kind of love God has blessed us with. Let's make God proud in our actions. Let's RISE together my Sistas!

Look out for Part 2 of "Love for Her Sistas"

May God bless you and your families!
Valencia Clay

www.ingramcontent.com/pod-product-compliance
Lightning Source LLC
LaVergne TN
LVHW010027070426
835510LV00001B/11